TESSELLATIONS
The History and Making of Symmetrical Designs

Written by Pam Stephens

Artwork by Jim McNeill

CrystalProductions

Aspen, Colorado   Glenview, Illinois

Library of Congress Control Number: 2003544760

ISBN 1-56290-243-1

Bonjour! My name is Paul LeGonn and this is my friend, Tess E. Lashun. We are your travel guides through the world of tessellation designs. On this journey you will learn all about tessellations and some artists who have made them. You'll also learn some things about math and history along the way. Later on, we'll show you how to make your own tessellations.

Are you ready to take this journey with us?

Then put on your thinking caps and lace up your travel shoes. Behind these doors are many places to go and lots of people to meet.

Welcome to the Tessellation Gallery! Have you ever been to a gallery before? A gallery is a place where artwork is on display. The Tessellation Gallery is the first stop on our journey. In the Tessellation Gallery you will see . . . what else? . . . tessellations.

What *is* a tessellation, you might be wondering?

Listen carefully.

A tessellation is a special kind of design. Some tessellations are simple and some tessellations are complex, but all tessellation designs follow certain rules.

Tessellations are made from different patterns of repeating shapes. The shapes that make up a tessellation are called polygons. Polygons are closed shapes that have three or more sides. Some examples of polygons are triangles, squares, and octagons. Polygons that are the exact same size are called congruent.

In tessellation designs, congruent polygons fit together like jigsaw puzzle pieces that repeat again and again. There are never any gaps between the shapes and the shapes never overlap each other. The design could go on forever.

Now that you know what a tessellation is, look very closely at the gallery. How many tessellations can you find? The answer might surprise you.

Did you see that there are three tessellations on the gallery walls?

Translation Lady is the title of the tessellation on the left wall. The tessellation on the right wall is titled *Rotation Rabbit*. On the back wall is a tessellation titled *Reflection Bird*. You will learn all about these different kinds of tessellations and how to make them later.

What other tessellations did you find? Did you notice the ceiling and floor? They are tessellations, too!

The ceiling design is made
with square shapes.

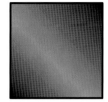

The floor design is made
with triangle shapes.

Both the ceiling and floor designs were made by placing
congruent shapes next to each other. There are no gaps
between the shapes. None of the shapes overlap.

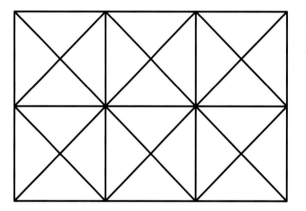

Although some of the shapes are light and some are dark, the shapes in
each design are congruent because they are exactly the same size.

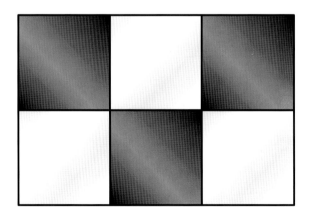

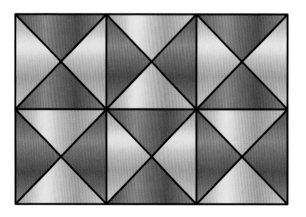

When shapes share congruent sides, they fit together like jigsaw puzzle pieces. They have no gaps between them and they never overlap each other.

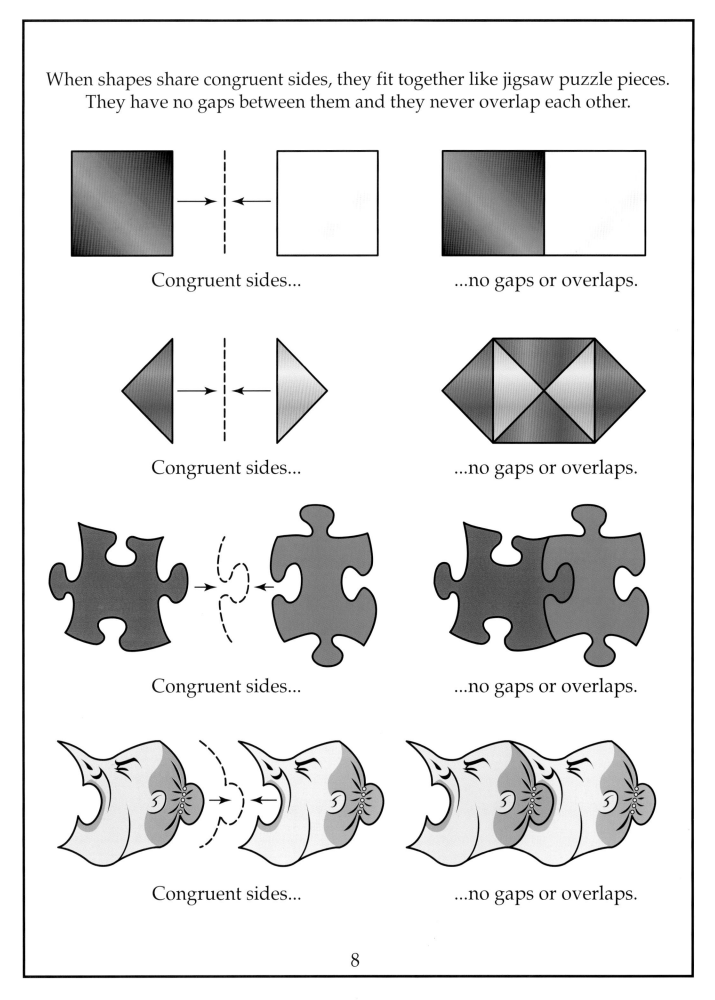

Congruent sides...

...no gaps or overlaps.

Congruent sides...

...no gaps or overlaps.

Congruent sides...

...no gaps or overlaps.

Congruent sides...

...no gaps or overlaps.

How do you like that, Tess? It's not often you can find art on walls, floors, and ceilings. We were walking on tessellations!

Speaking of walking on tessellations, did you know that the word "tessellation" comes from the old Latin word "tessella?" Tessella means tile. Because such an old language had a word for tessellations, we know that tessellations were created thousands of years ago. People from all around the world have been making tessellations for many centuries.

Are you ready to go to the History Gallery to see some tessellations from different times and places? I see that our ride is here. Let's go. . .

HISTORY
GALLERY

Whoa! Here we are at our first history stop.

Tessellation designs were first created more than 6000 years ago in Mesopotamia. Mesopotamia is what we now call the Middle East and was located in what we know as Iraq.

These original designs were made from pebbles set in plaster. They were simple designs used to decorate floors. As time passed, however, tessellation designs became more and more complex. Later designs were often created with clay mosaic tiles. The clay tiles were carefully painted with a design and then attached in repeating pattern to walls, floors, and ceilings.

Examples of early tessellations can be found in special places such as mosques and castles. A mosque is a place of worship. A castle is a large building with thick walls designed to protect the royal family or others who live in it.

Today, if you wish to see some famous tessellation designs you could visit Granada, Spain, to see the Alhambra. The Alhambra is a 700-year-old castle built by Moorish kings in the 1300s. Almost every surface of the Alhambra is covered with some sort of tessellation design made from mosaic tiles.

Look at the mosaic tile design on the next page. How many hours do you think it would take an artist to cover a whole wall with a design such as this?

Land ho! Our second history stop is the 1600s in the thirteen original American Colonies. These colonies later became the first states in the United States. As we look around, we do not see mosques or palaces. There are only log cabins and a few other small buildings.

Then where will we find tessellation designs in the Colonies? Tessellations were found in the homes of most early European settlers. Unlike the Alhambra, these early American designs were not on walls, floors, or ceilings. They were found covering the beds.

The first European settlers in the United States had hardly any places to buy items that they needed for day-to-day life. They could not be wasteful. When a dress or a pair of pants became too tattered to wear, the pieces of cloth that were still in good repair were saved for other uses. Often the smallest pieces of cloth were cut into shapes and sewn together to make patchwork quilts.

A quilt is a blanket-like bed covering made from three layers of fabric. The bottom layer of a quilt is usually plain. The middle layer is a filling of cotton, feathers, or some other material. The top layer is a decorative pattern. All three layers are stitched together. Many of the decorative patterns found on early American quilts are repeating designs of congruent shapes cut from small pieces of cloth.

Patchwork quilts are still made today. Many of the old designs are used in new quilts. The designs have names such as Bow Tie, Log Cabin, or Tumbling Blocks.

Look at the patchwork quilt design on the next page. Can you think of a name for this design? How is it similar to a mosaic tile design?

12

All aboard! Next history stop, Holland in 1898. This is the place and time that artist Maurits Cornelius Escher, who later became well known as M.C. Escher, was born. Escher was a graphic artist who is most responsible for making tessellation designs popular. Graphic artists are artists who create art through drawing, painting, printmaking, or other media.

During his career, Escher created many unusual artworks. He was especially interested in the way that his drawings could trick the viewer into seeing a flat picture as something three dimensional. The artwork for which Escher became famous, however, is tessellations.

After a visit to the Alhambra in 1920, Escher became captivated by the designs he saw there. He made many sketches while at the Alhambra. When he returned to his home, Escher began to make his own tessellated designs of fish, birds, and other objects. Because he understood the mathematical ideas involved with making different kinds of tessellations, Escher's artwork is often very complex.

What is even more interesting about M.C. Escher's work is that most of his tessellation designs are woodcut prints. To make a woodcut print, the design is cut away from a block of wood. Ink is then applied to the design and the block is pressed onto paper.

Look at the artwork on the next page. How is the background design similar to mosaic tile and patchwork quilt patterns?

Surf's up! Last history stop, almost any computer in the world.

We have learned that the oldest tessellations were simple designs made from pebbles set in plaster. Later, tessellations were painted on the tiles that covered walls of mosques, palaces, and castles. In the first American colonies, quilts were made with tessellation designs. Then a famous Dutch artist, M.C. Escher, made tessellation drawings and prints popular. Now we are about to discover another way that tessellations can be created in our time.

Technology has given artists a new way to make tessellations and to display them. By using a computer and special software, artists are able to draw tessellations, fill them with details, and add color. As soon as the tessellations are made, these artists are able to show them to the world by posting them to websites on the Internet. When artists place their computer-made tessellation designs on the Internet, people from around the world are able to see the designs anytime they wish.

Look at the tessellation design on the next page. This tessellation was first created to be the design for a magazine cover, then the artist placed it on his website for everyone to see.

How have the uses for tessellation designs changed through time?

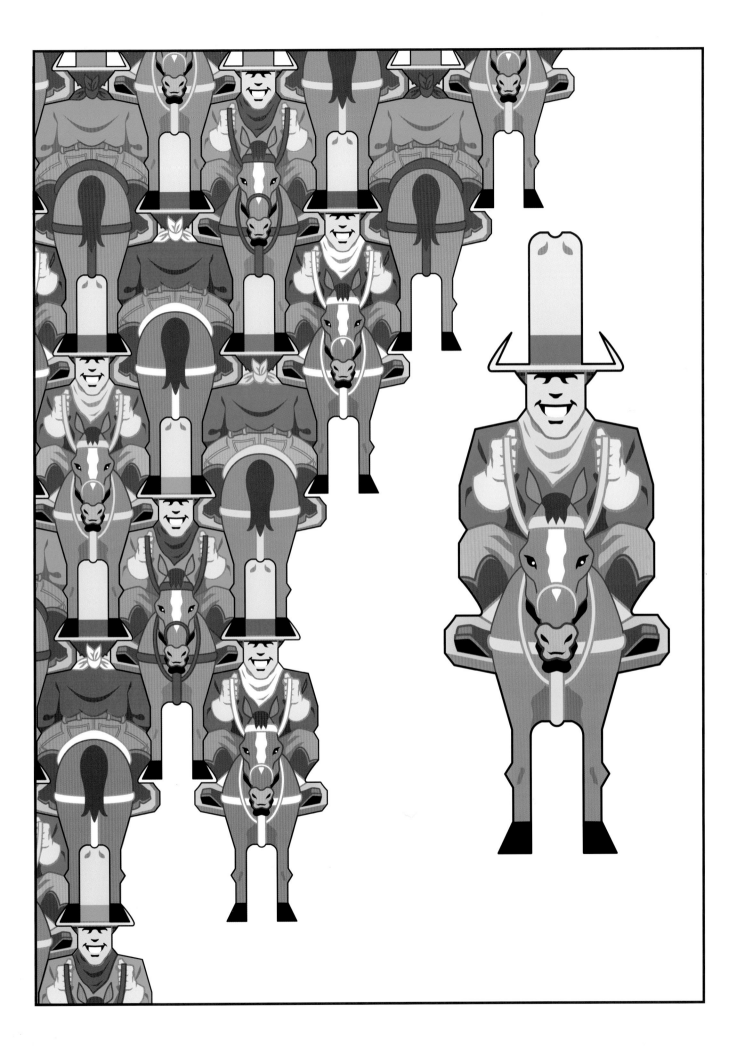

Now that you have met some artists and seen where and why tessellation designs have been created, are you ready to try your hand at making your own? Before you begin, you will need to collect all of these materials:

- Different colors of construction paper, 12" x 18"
- Pencil and eraser
- Scissors
- Glue
- Ruler (an 18-inch ruler works best)
- Tape
- Index cards with lines on them, 3" x 5"
- Markers, crayons, or colored pencils to add details

When you have these materials, the next step is to learn how to measure and draw a grid. A grid is a pattern of vertical and horizontal parallel lines. Vertical lines go up and down on the page. Horizontal lines go across the page. Parallel lines are side by side and never touch.

The grid you create will cover your page with three-inch squares. This grid will help to keep your tessellation design straight on the page and in the correct positions.

You will need to practice how to measure and mark your paper to create a grid. For practice, you may wish to use scrap paper instead of your construction paper. Follow the instructions on the next page to create a grid. Make sure that you understand how to create a perfect grid before you join us again in the Tessellation Gallery.

Place your ruler so that it is parallel to the top edge of the paper. The left end of your ruler should be even with the vertical edge of the paper. Find 3 inches, 6 inches, 9 inches, 12 inches, and 15 inches on your ruler. Place a tiny dot on your paper at each of these ruler marks. Now move your ruler closer to the bottom of the paper and mark the same places.

Place your ruler so that it touches the first dot at the top and bottom. Hold the ruler still and then lightly draw a straight line that connects the two dots. Connect the other dots the same way. You should have five straight, vertical lines when you are finished.

Next, place your ruler so that it is parallel to the left edge of your paper. Find 3 inches, 6 inches, and 9 inches on your ruler. Place a tiny dot on your paper at each of these ruler marks. Now move your ruler closer to the right vertical edge of your paper and mark the same places.

Place your ruler so that it touches the first and last dots on the top row. Hold your ruler still and then connect the two dots with a lightly drawn line from one edge of the paper to the other. Connect the other dots the same way. If you have made a perfect grid, let's go to the Tessellation Gallery now.

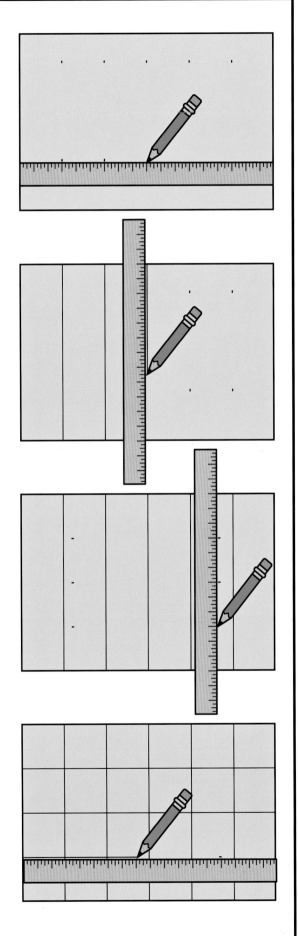

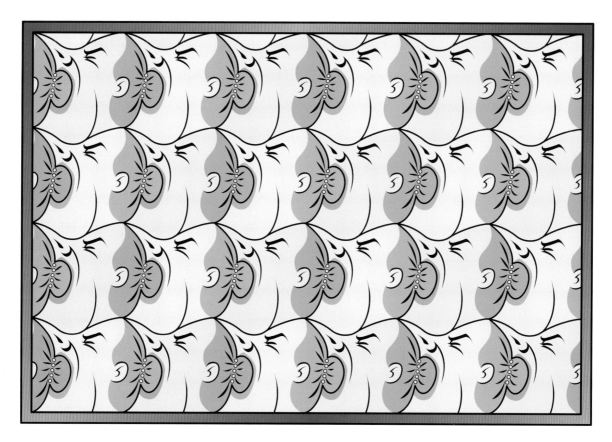

Welcome back to the Tessellation Gallery. We see you ve brought your art supplies and materials. You must be ready to learn about the types of tessellation designs and how they are made.

There are three basic types of tessellations. These types of tessellations are called translation, rotation, and reflection. The simplest type is called a translation. *Translation Lady* is this type of tessellation.

In a translation, the original shape is created then repeated again and again. The congruent shapes fit together like pieces of a jigsaw puzzle. The shapes never overlap and there are no gaps between them.

If you look closely at the translation tessellation on this page, you will see that the finished design is repeated in both a horizontal and a vertical pattern. Do you see how the design easily fits into a grid pattern?

To begin your own translation, you will need two different colors of construction paper. Each sheet of the paper should have a three-inch grid drawn on it. You also will need to measure and cut an index card into a three-inch square. Now follow the instructions that begin on the next page.

Draw a curved line from the top left corner to the top right corner of the index card.

Next, draw a different curved line from the top left corner to the bottom left corner.

Carefully cut along the lines you drew.

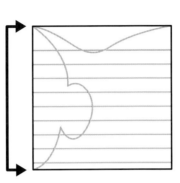

Slide the top shape to the bottom of the card. Make sure all of the lines are horizontal.

Tape the straight edge of the shape to the bottom edge of the card.

Slide the left side shape to the right side of the card. Make sure all of the lines are horizontal.

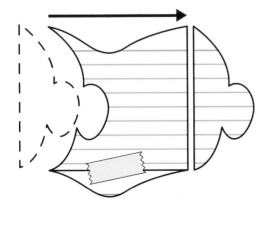

Tape the straight edge of the shape to the right edge of the card.

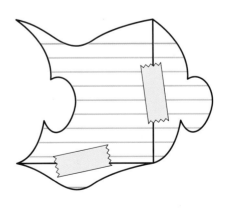

Place the cutout shape onto the top left square of one of the grids you have drawn. The straight edges of the index card should be placed on the straight edges of the square. Trace around the shape.

Slide the shape to the next grid space until it fits like a jigsaw puzzle piece with the first shape you traced. Trace the shape again.

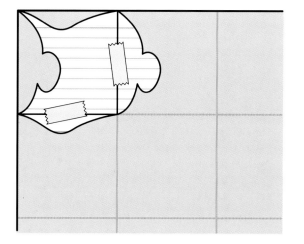

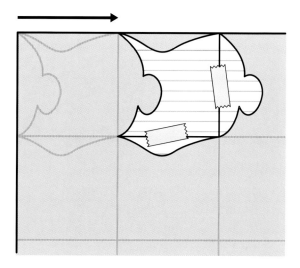

Repeat sliding and tracing until the entire grid is filled with the shape.

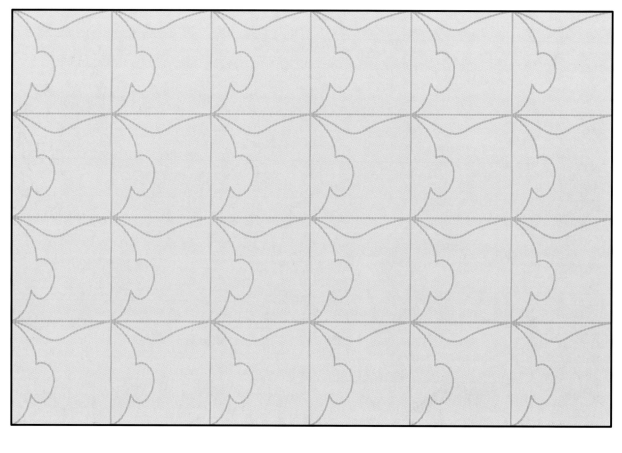

Carefully cut out all of the shapes you have drawn. Do not throw away any of the little pieces.

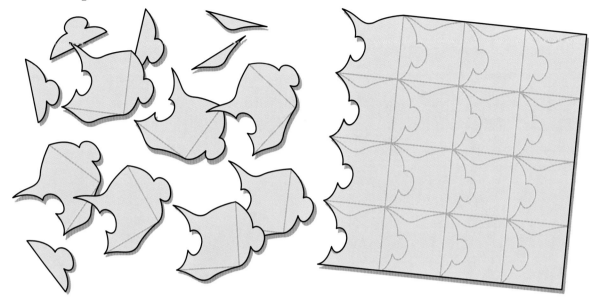

On your other grid, arrange the cutout shapes and glue them in a checkerboard pattern of congruent shapes. Erase any grid lines that show and then add details with markers, crayons, or colored pencils. (See the finished tessellation on page 20.)

Another type of tessellation design is called a rotation. *Rotation Rabbit* is this type of tessellation. In a rotation tessellation, the congruent shape is created then it is repeated around a central point.

If you look closely, you will see that the finished design is repeated in a circular pattern. Do you see how this design easily fits into a grid pattern?

To begin your own rotation tessellation, you will again need two sheets of construction paper. Each sheet should be a different color and have a three-inch grid drawn on it. Measure and cut an index card into a three-inch square then follow the instructions that begin on the next page.

Draw a curved line from the top left corner to the top right corner.

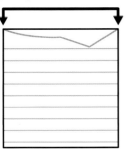

Draw a curved line from the top left corner to the bottom left corner.

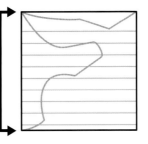

Carefully cut along the lines you have drawn.

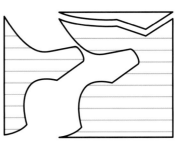

Swing the left shape to the bottom of your index card. Make sure that the lines on your cutout shape are vertical and the lines on your card are horizontal.

Tape the straight edge of the shape to the bottom edge of the card.

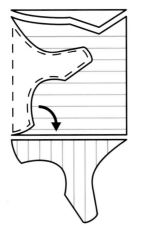

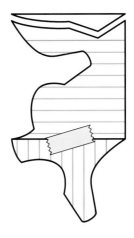

Swing the top shape to the right side of your index card. Make sure that the lines on your cutout shape are vertical and the lines on your card are horizontal.

Tape the straight edge of the shape to right edge of the card.

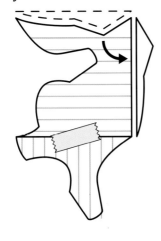

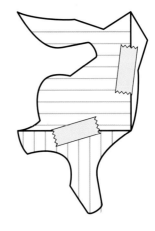

Place the shape you have created in the upper left corner of one of the grids. The corner of the index card should touch the corner of the paper. Trace around the shape.

Rotate the shape until its top edge fits like a jigsaw puzzle piece with the first shape you traced. The shapes cannot overlap. Some of the shape will go off of the paper. Trace around the apart of the shape that is on the paper.

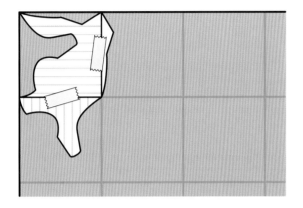

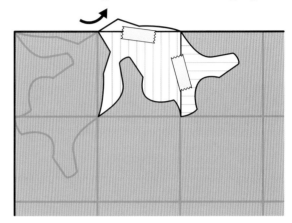

Now rotate the shape so that it fits like a jigsaw puzzle piece with the second tracing. Trace the shape again.

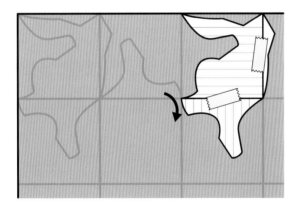

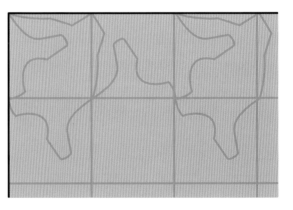

Continue this pattern until the top row is filled with congruent shapes that do not overlap.

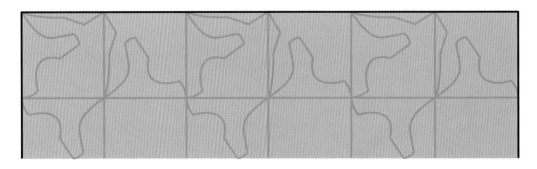

Begin a second row of shapes.
Place the shape so that it fits like a
jigsaw puzzle piece with the first
tracing on the top row. Some of
the shape will go off of the paper.
Trace around the shape.

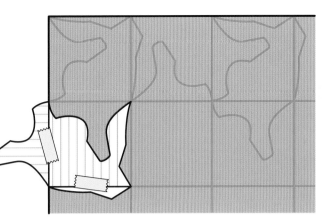

Rotate the shape until it fits like a
jigsaw puzzle piece with the top
row and the tracing you just
made. Make sure the shapes do
not overlap. Trace the shape.

Rotate the shape again until it fits
like a jigsaw puzzle piece with the
top row and the tracing you just
made. None of the tracings should
overlap. Trace the shape.

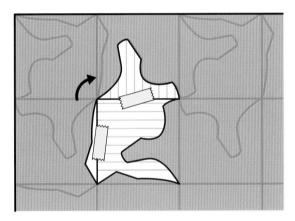

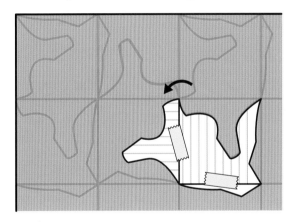

Continue rotating the shape until it fits like a jigsaw puzzle piece and trace.
Fill the page with tracings of the congruent shape.

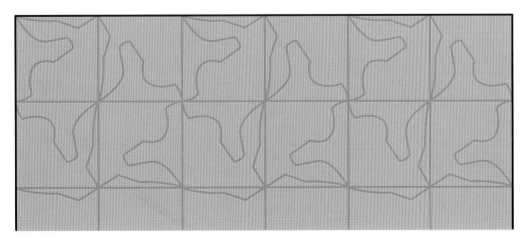

Carefully cut out the shapes your have traced. Do not throw away any of the pieces.

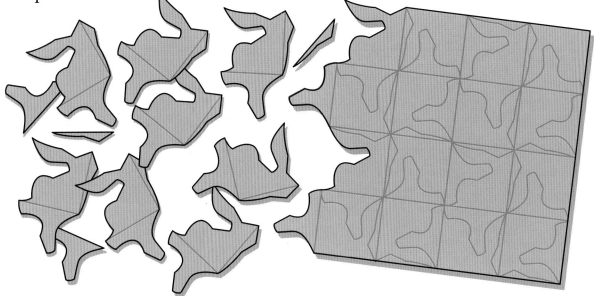

On the other grid, arrange the cutout shapes and glue them in a checkerboard pattern of congruent shapes. Erase any grid lines that show. Add details with markers, crayons, or colored pencils. (See the finished tessellation on page 24.)

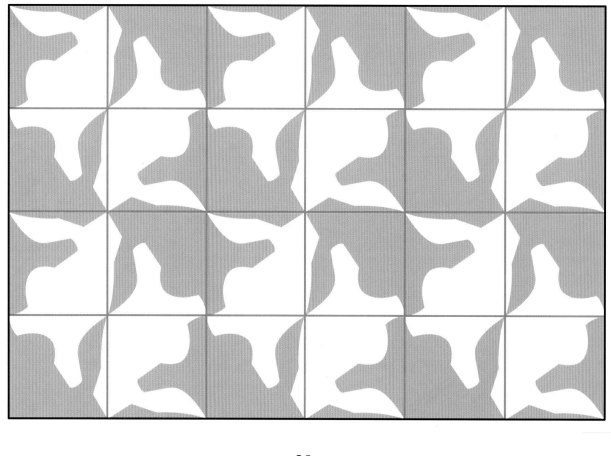

The third type of tessellation is called a reflection. *Reflection Bird* is this type of tessellation.

Just like a translation and a rotation, a reflection tessellation is created from an original shape that is repeated again and again. The congruent shapes fit together like jigsaw puzzle pieces.

What makes a reflection different is that the original shape is repeated in a pattern that places some of the congruent shapes backwards on the page. It's as if the shape was looking in a mirror at itself! Look at the reflection tessellation on this page. Do you see the original shape? Now find the same shape flipped and repeated backwards. Do you see that reflection tessellations fit easily into a grid?

To begin your own reflection tessellation, you will need two sheets of construction paper. Each sheet should be a different color and have a three-inch grid drawn on it. Measure and cut an index card into a three-inch square, then follow the instructions that start on the next page.

Draw a curved line from the top left corner to the top right corner of the index card.

Next, draw a different curved line from the top left corner to the bottom left corner.

Carefully cut along the lines you drew.

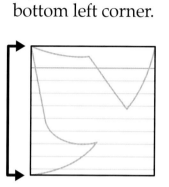

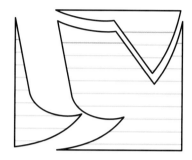

Slide the top shape to the bottom of the index card. Make sure all of the lines are horizontal.

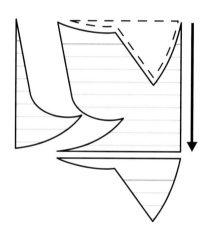

Flip the shape over so the lines are on the back of the shape. Tape the straight edge of the shape to the bottom edge of the index card.

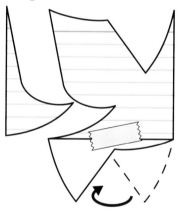

Slide the left shape to the right side of the index card.

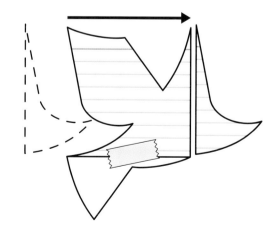

Flip the shape over so that the lines are on the back of the shape. Tape the straight edge of the shape to the right edge of the card.

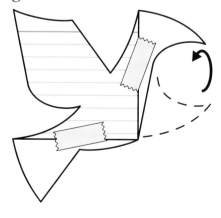

Place the shape you have made in the upper left corner of one of the grids. Be sure that the original straight edges of the index card fit along the lines of the grid. Carefully trace around the shape.

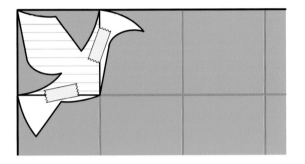

Flip the shape to its backside. Some of the shape will go off of the page. When the congruent shapes fit together like jigsaw puzzle pieces, trace around the shape again.

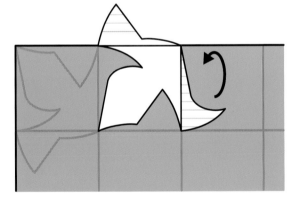

Slide the shape into the next grid space. The shape will not fit like a jigsaw puzzle piece yet.

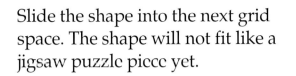

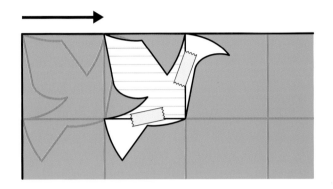

Flip the shape and slide it to the next grid space until the congruent shapes fit together like jigsaw puzzle pieces. Trace around the shape again.

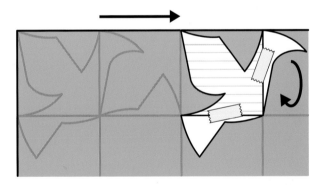

Continue sliding, flipping, and tracing until the top row is filled with congruent shapes.

Return the cutout shape to the upper left corner of the grid. Make sure that the cutout shape fits exactly onto the first traced shape.

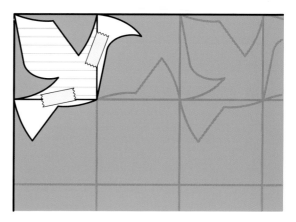

Slide the shape down to the next row. The cutout shape will not fit like a jigsaw puzzle piece until you flip it over to face in the opposite direction.

Some of the shape will go off of the page. Carefully trace around the shape.

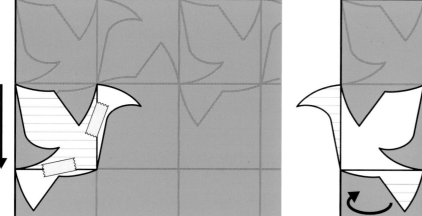

Continue to slide, flip, and trace the congruent shapes until the whole page is filled. Make sure none of the shapes overlap and that there are no spaces between them.

Carefully cut out all of the shapes you have traced onto the grid.
Do not throw away any of the little pieces.

On the second grid, arrange the cutout shapes in a checkerboard pattern.
Glue the shapes to the grid and add details with markers, crayons, or colored
pencils. (See the finished tessellation on page 29.)

You have now tried your hand at making three types of tessellations. Although all three kinds of tessellations use congruent shapes that fit together like jigsaw puzzle pieces, you learned that each tessellation repeats in a special way.

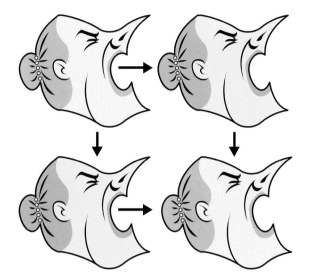

Translations repeat in a side-to-side and top-to-bottom pattern of congruent shapes.

Rotations repeat in a circle pattern of congruent shapes.

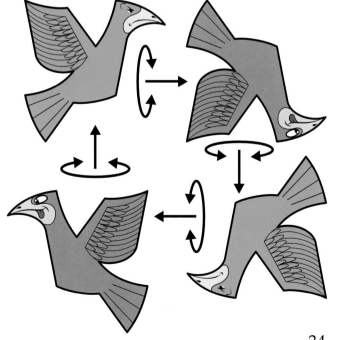

Reflections repeat in a side-to-side or top-to-bottom and backwards pattern of congruent shapes.

Now, let s look at another way artists can create tessellations.

Sometimes the patterns in tessellations are easy to find, but sometimes an artist can trick you. In this tessellation, titled *Escher Bowl*, can you find the congruent shape that is repeated again and again?

If you found that the congruent shape is the outline of two football players together, you are right!

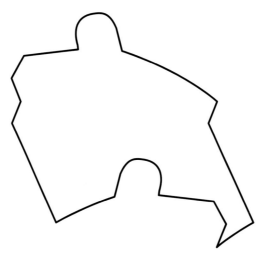

Do you see that each pair of football players is shaped exactly like all the others? Only the details inside of the shapes are different.

The congruent shapes repeat as a translation from side to side and as a reflection from top to bottom.

Look closely at the outlines in this tessellation design. Can you decide what kind of repetition is used? Do you have an idea about what the outline shapes could be? Turn the page to find out.

Voilà! Did you see? It's a side-to-side translation and a top-to-bottom reflection of us, Tess and Paul! We hope that you have enjoyed your journey with us!

Glossary

Bonjour A French word that means "hello"

Complex Complicated, not simple

Congruent Polygons that are the same size and shape

Design The arrangement of the parts of an artwork

Grid A regularly repeating pattern of horizontal and vertical lines

Horizontal Side to side and parallel to the horizon

Mosaic A design made from stone, glass, ceramic, or paper tiles that is attached to a surface such as a wall, floor, ceiling, or canvas with concrete, mortar, or glue

Parallel Lines that are side by side and never touch

Pattern A design created from art elements in a regular manner

Polygon A closed plane figure made with three or more lines

Reflection A repeating tessellated shape that mirrors itself

Repetition To use the same art element again and again in a work of art

Rotation A tessellated shape that repeats around a point

Tessellation A design created by congruent shapes that cover a surface without any of the shapes overlapping each other or having gaps between them

Three-dimensional A form that has or seems to have height, width, and depth

Tile A repeating design that covers an entire surface

Translation A tessellated shape that can repeat in a vertical and horizontal pattern

Two-dimensional Artwork that is flat

Vertical Up and down

Voilà A French word to suggest an appearance as if by magic

About the Author and the Artist

Photo by Bob Stephens.

Author Pam Stephens lives and works in North Texas. She is an art specialist in the Hurst-Euless-Bedford Independent School District. Her education includes a BFA from Midwestern State University in addition to an MA and a Ph.D. in art education from the University of North Texas. She has co-authored a study print series for Crystal Productions, Take 5 Interdisciplinary Connections, and one book, *Bridging the Curriculum through Art*, with Nancy Walkup. Additionally Pam has published classroom art games, teacher resource guides for art museums, and numerous articles in professional journals and magazines. Pam is a frequent presenter at the Texas and National Art Education Association conferences.

Artist Jim McNeill lives and works in New Jersey. He is a freelance graphic artist whose clients include Popular Science, Macy's, and Egghead Software. Jim holds a BFA from the School of Visual Arts, New York City. His tessellation, *Escher Bowl*, is included in the Crystal Productions Take 5 study print set, *Interdisciplinary Connections: Art and Mathematics*. Jim went on to make Crystal's award-winning demonstration video, *Tessellations: How to Create Them*, and served as consultant for their tessellation demonstration poster set. His work has been exhibited in Feria Internacional del Mueble de Valencia's Atlas exposition in Valencia, Spain. Jim often presents workshops in school districts as well as at state and national art education conferences.

Tessellations: The History and Making of Symmetrical Designs is an online collaboration between the author and artist. The book was almost entirely written through electronic communication over a period of about one year.

Pam and Jim wish to thank Nancy Walkup for serving as editor on this project.